T0340493

CATS

IN

HATS

ROJIMAN & UMATAN

CATS IN HATS

Make Cat-Hair Headgear
for Your Feline Friends

Translated by Ian Fabian

Illustrations by Marisa Kwek

PAVILION

CONTENTS

INTRODUCTION

Hello to everyone reading this book! We (umatan and rojiman) are a cat-loving couple from Japan who make hats for our cats. We use the hair shed by our family cats Maru (a white cat), Mugi (an orange tabby) and Nya (a blue-grey tabby who sadly left this world in 2020). Yes, what you see on these cats' heads are hats made out of their own cat hair.

It all started in the summer of 2016, while umatan was brushing one of our cats, as she usually does. After removing the cat hair from the brush and piling it all up, it started looking like a mountain. Rubbing the hairs together on this little mountain made it taller and look like a radio tower. Feeling mischievous, umatan gently placed the radio tower on our cat's head, and the cat sat there, relaxed, with a composed look on his face. She was astonished by how cute and funny it looked.

At that moment, umatan realized that she could take the excess hair generated by our cats and, by rubbing it together, form any shape she wanted. The hair is so light that the cats don't mind when it's put on their heads. Cats have an excellent sense of smell, so they're probably comfortable with us putting their own hair on their heads because it smells like them.

Since then, we've made more than 160 different hats. Our cats provide us with their extra hair, umatan makes the hats and rojiman takes the photos. Making these hats has become our life's work and allows our whole family to come together.

Shedding is a headache for most cat owners. But once you learn how to make hats with cat hair, all that extra hair will become near and dear to you – and your cat can become as fashionable as your imagination allows. This book will show you how to make twenty-five cat-hair hats along with some basic techniques to create your own custom designs. We hope you have fun making these hats with your cat!

CAT-HAT ADVICE

When making hats for your cat, there are a few things that are helpful to know. In this section we offer brushing advice; explain the best ways to collect, clean and store cat hair; list recommended tools; describe how to accommodate cat ears of different sizes; discuss some ways to help make your cat comfortable wearing hats; and give tips for getting the best photos of your cat in hats.

The Best Way to Brush a Cat

Removing hair with a brush is good for your cat. Brushing helps prevent cats from swallowing too much fur, which can accumulate in their stomach and form hairballs. Regular brushing is also a good opportunity for you to check the condition of your cat's skin and fur as well as the cat's weight, muscles and fat, to make sure your pet is healthy. Above all else, it's a great way to bond with your cat, so get into the habit of brushing regularly!

At our house, before we brush our cats we ask them, 'Is it all right if we brush you?' while petting their heads and scratching their necks. After massaging their entire bodies and making them feel good, we then start using the brush.

If your cat pulls or runs away while you brush, they're definitely not in the mood – so wait and try again another time. For cats that hate being brushed, we recommend petting them using one hand while applying the brush with your other hand and brushing little by little. Most cats dislike being brushed on their bellies and legs, so if these spots annoy your cat, avoid them.

There are all kinds of brushes out there. Try out different kinds to find one that your cat will like!

How to Collect Enough Cat Hair

The amount and quality of hair your cat sheds depends on the cat. We have been collecting and storing cat hair for several years now, so making big hats is not a problem for us. But if you're just starting out and don't have much cat hair, you can still make small hats that look really cute (see page 9). Over time, you will eventually gather enough cat hair to make larger hats.

If your cat's hair is only one colour, you may have a bit of trouble designing some of the multicoloured hats. In these situations, you can use adhesive-backed felt sheets or some yarn to add different-coloured highlights. Make sure your cat doesn't eat these when feeling mischievous!

Be careful if you're using cat hair from another cat outside of your home, such as a neighbour or friend's cat. Make sure that the other cat does not have any pre-existing skin conditions, fleas, ticks or lice. Also, cats can be territorial, so the smell of another cat's hair may stress out your cat. If you still want to try using hair from another cat, make sure to wash the hair first (see page 6) and then let your cat smell the hair to see the reaction.

Recycling Cat Hair

Cat hair is a limited resource, so we recycle it by taking apart old
hats and reusing the hair to make new ones. We don't make the
cat hair harden like wool felt and we don't use any adhesive in
our hats, so the hats are easily broken down. If the hair has been
washed and you store it properly (see page 6), it can actually
keep for a long time. It's been five years since we started saving
our cats' hair, and our stored hair is still fluffy and usable. We
cherish this special textile that only our cats can provide.

How to Clean & Store Cat Hair

Cat saliva, dandruff and hair contain proteins that can cause allergies in some people, and washing the hair can reduce the level of these allergens. In addition, we assume that the hair you are collecting to make these hats has no fleas, ticks or lice, but as an extra precaution – especially with cats that like to roam and play outside – you may want to wash the hair in boiling water instead of lukewarm to help remove any pests that are present.

Here are the steps for washing and drying cat hair:

1. Pour lukewarm water into a bucket, bowl or sink, and mix in some cat shampoo (available at pet stores or online).

2. Spread the cat hair flat in a mesh basket that will fit into the bucket, bowl or sink.

3. Dip the basket into the water and gently shake the hairs to wash them. Do not scrub or rub the hairs too roughly or they may mat together and become like felt.

4. Rinse the cat hair well with lukewarm water.

5. Remove the remaining water from the cat hair by blotting it with an old towel.

6. Place the cat hair in a zippered mesh laundry bag and hang it until the hair dries completely.

7. Once completely dry, use your fingers to untangle the hairs and leave them as fluffy as you can.

1 2 3

If you wash too much cat hair at once, it will clump together, making it much more difficult to dry and untangle. Therefore, it's important to wash the hair in small enough batches that you can keep the hair fairly flat and in a single layer. Very long cat hair is also difficult to untangle; cutting the collected hair with scissors before washing it will make it much easier to handle.

When storing dry cat hair for later use, make sure to keep the hair in a breathable container. In our home, we use boxes made from paulownia (princess tree) wood, which is said to repel insects and to have antifungal properties.

Recommended Tools

Making cat-hair hats does not require fancy tools. Here are a few essential tools and some non-essential but handy items to get you started.

Essential Tools

Sewing needles

Thread of a colour similar to your cat's coat

Scissors

Dressmaking or straight pins

Felting needles

Non-woven pleated face mask to prevent breathing in cat hair while you work

Other Handy Items

10-cm (4-inch) foam half-spheres for the tops of hat stands and for making the basic **Cup** shape (page 14)

Empty glass jars for the base of hat stands

Sticky tape for attaching foam half-spheres to jars to make hat stands and for making cardboard or paper moulds

Adhesive-backed felt sheets for adding different colours (see 'how to collect enough cat hair', page 4)

Long darning needles for making it easier to sew thick parts together

Cardboard for making moulds for the birthday cake (page 61), cheesehead (page 91), coonskin cap (page 95) and top hat (page 123), and for making a finger guard (see 'reinforcing edges', page 19)

Felting mat or dishwashing sponge, for protecting the work surface while reinforcing edges

Felting tool that holds three parallel felting needles flat in a straight line, for reinforcing edges

Different-Sized Cat Ears & Heads

Most of the hats in this book should be large enough to fit with your cat's ears comfortably inside but if not, make hats with incisions for the ears or smaller hats that will fit on top of your cat's head in between the ears.

To make a small hat, pack the hair into a mould that resembles the hat. For example, a single-serving yogurt pot works well for a little Top Hat.

In particular, these hat designs make very good small hats: Acorn hat (page 15), Unicorn (page 55), Halloween Witch hat (page 73), Santa Claus (page 77), Propeller Beanie (page 111), Sherlock Holmes (page 119) and Top Hat (page 123).

The sizes of all the parts provided in this book are those that fit our cats' heads. Each cat has a slightly different head size, so please adjust the final sizes to fit your cat.

How to Make Your Cat Comfortable Wearing Hats

Whenever your cat is relaxed, that's your chance to put a hat on. First, pet your cat's head while using a reassuring voice. If the cat is in a good mood, gently place the hat on. If your cat snarls, hisses or growls, it's a sign that the cat doesn't feel like wearing a hat. You can always try again some other time.

When you show a hat to your cat, they may put their nose out to sniff the hat. Let your cat smell the hat as much as they please, since they are probably trying to reassure themselves that the hat is not dangerous.

You can also place hats on cats' heads while they are sleeping. These hats only weigh about 10 grams (¼ oz), so most cats will hardly notice them.

Make sure to remove the hat as soon as you've taken your photos. But remove the hat carefully, because these hats will quickly become disfigured if they fall off your cat's head or if you grab them forcefully. Never leave your cats unattended with the hats or with any decorative collars, such as Amelia Earhart (page 87), Jester (page 103) or Queen (page 115), which could be choking hazards.

If your cat wears the hat with no fuss, make sure to offer lots of praise. Don't forget to give some treats as a reward. If done properly, you and your cat will find it fun to wear all these hats!

Cats wearing hats is only possible if you have a trusting relationship with your cat. If your cat seems reluctant about having a hat on, stop right there. Make sure never to force your cat to wear a hat and, instead, try to be in harmony with your cat's overall mood.

How to Take Better Photos of Your Cat

When taking photos of your cat wearing hats, having two people on hand makes the process more manageable. One person acts as the photographer, while the other takes care of the hat and encourages the cat to look in the right direction by making noises or motions off camera. The hats will often fall off your cat's head and can become deformed, so it's also important to have someone there to try to catch the hats carefully before they hit the floor.

It's essential to know your pet's behavioural patterns. By doing so, you will understand when your cat feels relaxed and when is a good time for wearing a hat. As for our cats, the best opportunity we have to take photos is early in the morning, by the window.

Take advantage of cats' natural habit of getting into boxes or lying on mats as a convenient way to attract them to – or move them to – a spot that's best for a photo shoot. Place a box or mat in specific areas of your home, and your cat will naturally come to these objects and start relaxing. If the box or mat is in a good location for photography, you can begin! If not, and your cat allows, you can conveniently move the box or mat with the cat in/on it to a more suitable position for shooting.

If you take photos of cat-hair hats in direct sunlight, the hair may be over-exposed and it won't make for a clear shot. We recommend using early morning sunlight or soft natural lighting through translucent curtains in order to see the soft, fluffy texture of the hats.

We also recommend taking photos for a short period of time rather than an extended photo shoot. Shorter periods reduce the burden on your cat.

Do photo shoots at different times of the day and with various backgrounds in order to change the mood of your photos – even when using the same hat.

Finally, placing some of the hats slightly askew on the cat's head can make for some really cute looks!

BASIC SHAPES & TECHNIQUES

The following shapes and techniques are used in many of the hats in this book, so let's master them.

THE CUP

The most fundamental shape is the **Cup**, which allows the hat to fit on the cat's head. For our cats, the cup is about 10 cm (4 inches) in diameter and 5 cm (2 inches) in height. Every cat's head size is different, though, so you'll want to adjust the cup size to fit your cat.

To make the cup:

1. Roll loose cat hair lightly into a ball about the size of a fist.

2. Push the centre in with your thumb to make a dent for the cat's head to fit.

3. Press the concave side (inside of the cup) with your fist or a foam half-sphere and stroke the surface while rotating it.

4. Add hair to the convex surface (outside of the cup) and rub it in with your palms to harden and stabilize the hair. Repeat steps 3 and 4 if needed to make the cup bigger and adjust it to your cat's head size. A stable thickness is about 1 cm (⅜ inch).

5. Wrap the fuzzy part of the cup's edge with some cat-hair **Gauze** (page 16), and carefully rub it in to produce a nice clean edge.

6. Finish by rubbing the entire surface to smooth it out.

Acorn hat

Beret

Variations

Acorn hat: Using a dressmaking pin, lift the hair on the top of the cup up into a point.

Beret: Squish the cup a bit into the shape of a beret. Make a ball that is about 3 cm (1¼ inches) across and fasten it on the top of the cup by poking the base of the ball into the cup several times with a felting needle. You can use different-coloured hair for the ball.

3

4

5

6

GAUZE

Gauze is a thin sheet of cat hair used to cover and smooth out fuzzy areas, or to add different patterns and colours (if using different-coloured cat hair) to your hats. If you only have cat hair of a single colour available, feel free to use adhesive-backed felt sheets instead of gauze to add different colours to your hats (see photo, opposite).

To make and apply gauze:

(1) Rub some cat hair while holding it flat in between the palms of your hands. The hairs will intertwine and form a thin, gauze-like sheet.

(2) **A** If using the gauze to cover and smooth out a fuzzy area, lay a thin sheet of gauze on top of the rough area. (See also 'Reinforcing Edges', page 19.)

B If using the gauze or adhesive-backed felt sheets to add different patterns and colours to a hat, such as the inside of an animal ear, cut a pattern out of paper and make sure it fits the space on the hat. For the inside of ears, cut a shape that is slightly smaller than the ears you made. Use the paper pattern to cut the shape out of the gauze or felt sheet.

(3) To apply the gauze to the hat, rub the gauze into the desired surface with your fingertips. For thin gauze, just rubbing it is usually sufficient to attach it; for extra stability, though, you can poke the gauze about five times with a felting needle.

(1)

Variation

For hats that need a thicker gauze, such as for the Elephant ears (page 35), the mortarboard of the Graduation Cap (page 69) and the brims of the Halloween Witch hat (page 73) and Top Hat (page 123), continue adding more hair to the thin gauze sheet made in Step 1 and rub between your palms with each addition to entangle the fibres, harden the gauze and thicken the sheet.

STRING

Cat-hair **String** can be used in many situations where a thin or thick cylindrical piece is needed. To make it, simply roll some hair back and forth between your palms to form a string.

Different types of string include:

(1) **Stiff String** If you need a stiff string, such as for the Snail tentacles (page 51) or the Birthday Cake candle (page 61), rub the string harder and apply more pressure when rolling until it is firm.

(2) **Flat String** If you need a ribbon, like the crown's band on the Queen hat (page 115), squish a piece of string so it's flattened.

(3) **Fluffy String** If you need a fluffy string, such as for the manes of the Lion (page 43) or Unicorn (page 55) or for the Queen's hair (page 115), add more hair and roll it loosely.

(4) **Thick String** If you need a thick string, like those used for the Elephant trunk (page 35), the Sheep horns (page 47) or the raccoon tail on the Coonskin Cap (page 95), continue to add more hair and roll it in until you reach the desired thickness.

(5) **Short & Long String** Small thin strings, like those used for the Koala ears (page 39), can be made by using less hair; long strings, such as those in the plaits of the Queen hat (page 115) and Viking Helmet (page 127), are made with more hair.

REINFORCING EDGES

If the edges of flat parts, such as the Elephant ears or hat brims, are thin or fuzzy, they will start to tear unless you reinforce them.

To reinforce an edge:

(1) Make a protective guard for your finger by taking a piece of cardboard that is approximately 10 by 5 cm (4 by 2 inches), folding it around your index fingertip, and taping it closed.

(2) If the edge of the hat part is thin or was cut with scissors, wrap a thin sheet of **Gauze** (page 16) over the fuzzy edge of the hat part. This is recommended because edges cut with scissors are difficult for the felting needle to pierce.

(3) Place the hat part on a flat surface on top of a felting mat, hard dishwashing sponge or thick piece of cardboard. Hold the edge of the part down using your covered index finger, and poke the edge horizontally with a felting needle until firm. If you can find a felting tool that holds three parallel felting needles flat in a straight line, it makes the job faster and easier.

1

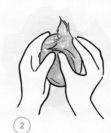

2

3

ATTACHING PARTS

Large parts, such as ears or horns, are attached to the cup or hat base by using a sewing needle and some thread that matches the colour of your cat's coat. Be careful how much force you apply with your hands, because a cat-hair hat is easily broken. You should not grab the cup or hat base as you sew – only gently support it.

To attach parts to a hat:

(1) Determine where to attach the parts to the cup or hat base, and adjust the connection point of the parts so that they fit cleanly on the surface of the cup or hat base. If there is a lot of excess hair, you may cut it off with scissors.

(2) Before sewing, there's no need to knot the thread. Start sewing from the inside of the cup or hat base and, as you pull the thread through, leave about 5 cm (2 inches) of thread hanging down on the inside.

(3) Proceed to sew on the part. (Rough-looking stitches are fine, since you will hide the seams later.)

(4) When you finish, end inside the cup or hat base and leave about 5 cm (2 inches) of the end of the thread hanging down, cutting off any excess along with the needle. You'll now have both ends of the thread hanging loose on the inside of the hat.

(5) In place of a knot, rub the loose ends of the thread into the bowl of the cup or hat base with your fingertips to anchor the thread and prevent it from slipping. If the attached part is still wobbly, you can use a standard square knot to tightly tie together the two ends of the thread.

(6) For a smooth finish, hide the seams and joints on the outside of the hat (see page 22).

(1)

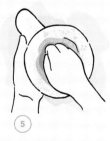

HIDING SEAMS & JOINTS

Sewing parts onto a hat sometimes creates small indentations, or seams, where the surface is pulled by the thread. Sewing also leaves noticeable joints between parts such as animal ears and the cup. When you are finished sewing, you can hide the seams and joints by applying cat hair like putty to get smooth, beautifully finished hats.

To hide seams:

(1) Cut some cat hair into small pieces, about the length of your fingertip (5 mm [³⁄₁₆ inch]).

(2) Cover the seams with the short hairs.

(3) Rub the area with your fingertips. Repeat, adding and rubbing hair in as needed until the surface looks smooth.

To hide a joint:

(1) Prepare a piece of **Gauze** (page 16) that is slightly larger than the joint.

(2) Cover the joint with the gauze.

(3) Rub the area with your fingertips. Poking the area about five times with a felting needle will further anchor the patch and prevent any hair from falling off.

To hide seams:

To hide a joint:

FINISHING TOUCHES

In the process of making a cat-hair hat, you will naturally leave a lot of dents and finger marks all over the hat. And because the material is so soft, the hat will inevitably deform as you work. So, wait until the very end and then fix everything up nicely as your final step.

To make finishing touches:

(1) Reposition attached parts by sticking a dressmaking pin into the base of the part and using it to move the part little by little. (This only works for slight adjustments, not major ones.)

(2) Fix finger marks and dents by inserting the tip of a dressmaking pin into the dent and lifting the hair up slowly. Then gently stroke the area with your hand to blend the hair in and smooth the surface.

(3) Use scissors to cut off excess hair that sticks out of the hat, making the outline of the hat more crisp and clean.

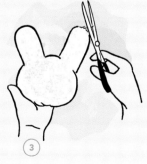

ANIMAL

HATS

Cats that morph into other animals are
hilarious and look cute enough to make anyone
laugh. In this chapter, we will guide you through
the special characteristics of various animals so that
you can create hats with animal motifs. You can
customize the look and feel of each hat by varying
the sizes and positions of the ears and horns.

BIRD WINGS

This is a beautiful hat made with wings that extend upwards. The wings require many parts that may be difficult to handle or manipulate, but if you sew them as if you were skewering them with the needle and thread, the wing shape will be stable. Find the best angle for the wings by turning them up a bit or spreading them out.

To best capture the wing shape when taking photos, use natural lighting near a window and guide your cat's eyes to look off to the side.

(1) Make the basic **Cup** shape (page 14).

(1)

Bird Wings *continued*

(2) To make a brim for the hat, lengthen a cat-hair **String** (page 18) so that it is long enough to loop once around the cup.

(3) Wrap the brim around the cup and sew it in place (see 'Attaching Parts', page 20).

(4) Reshape the cup if it has become deformed, and poke any fuzzy areas with a felting needle to shape the hat.

(5) To construct the wings, make two cat-hair strings that are 20 cm (8 inches) long and eight strings that are 15 cm (6 inches) long. You don't want the wings to lose their shape, so rub the strings firmly so that they harden.

(6) Bend the 20-cm (8-inch) strings, which will act as the wing's bone portion, into an L shape. Lay the ends of four 15-cm (6-inch) strings on the short leg of each L so that the line of the wing tip is diagonal (see photo, opposite). To achieve a diagonal with the tips, some of the opposite ends may protrude beyond the short leg of the L, but don't worry about that for now.

(7) Sew the 15-cm (6-inch) strings to the short leg of each L, and then further secure the wing parts together by skewering them with thread at intervals so that they don't fall apart.

(8) Use scissors to cut off any portion of the 15-cm (6-inch) strings that protrudes from the short leg of the L. Poke any extra fuzzy parts of the wings with a felting needle to control fluffing.

(9) Sew the wings onto the left and right sides of the cup. If you want the angle of the wings to be adjustable during photo shoots, only sew the base of the wings onto the cup. If you want the wings to be more stable, sew them on more fully against the sides of the cup.

COW

This hat is made to resemble a Holstein, or dairy cow. If you add some large horns that stick out in front of the hat, you can make your cat into a bull and pretend to be a bullfighter!

When designing an animal hat, we look at pictures of the animal as well as illustrations and stuffed animals for ideas and inspiration, and we encourage you to do the same.

1. Prepare the basic **Cup** shape (page 14).

1

(2)   (3)   (4)   (5)

Cow *continued*

(2) To make the ears, hold some cat hair with both hands and roll it into a ball that is about 6 cm (2½ inches) across.

(3) Crush the ball flat into a 10-cm (4-inch) circle, rubbing it in between your palms.

(4) Cut the flat circle in half with scissors so that you have two semi-circles.

(5) Make two thick cat-hair **Strings** (page 18) and shape them into curved horns. To give the hat a balanced look, try to make the horns about the same height as the semi-circular ears.

(6) To make the nose, create a ball and shape it into an oval. The total length of the oval should be about one-third the diameter of the cup.

(7) For the eyes and nostrils, make four small balls and shape them into ellipses; the eyes should be slightly larger than the nostrils. Try not to make these shapes too stiff, since it will become difficult later to attach them to the cup with a felting needle. (If you don't have different-coloured cat hair, you can use adhesive-backed felt sheets or substitute buttons for the eyes and nostrils.)

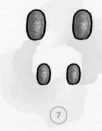

(6)   (7)

(8) Affix the nostrils made in Step 7 onto the nose from Step 6 with a felting needle.

(9) Sew the nose onto the cup (see 'Attaching Parts', page 20).

(10) Fold the semi-circular ears in half and sew them onto the cup with the crease facing up and outwards.

(11) Sew the horns onto the cup. If you bend the horns inwards just a bit, the hat will definitely look more like a cow.

(12) Affix the eyes made in Step 7 onto the cup using a felting needle.

(13) If necessary, hide the seams and joints of all the attached parts (see 'Hiding Seams & Joints', page 22).

(14) To create a cow's spotted pattern, make some **Gauze** (page 16), cut it into blotch-like shapes with scissors, and attach the shapes to the cup.

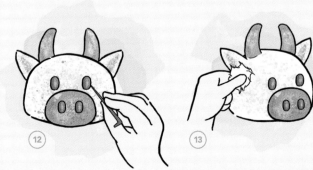

ELEPHANT

For hats with parts that extend below the cup, like this one, it is helpful to use a homemade hat stand when assembling them (see 'Recommended Tools', page 8).

Due to the big ears and trunk, the Elephant hat can be difficult to make and balance on your cat's head. When a hat you have worked so hard to make falls off your cat's head and is damaged, it's very upsetting, so during the photo shoot, ask your cat to stay still for a minute. Also, take the photo slightly from the side instead of head on, so that you can see the curvature of the trunk.

 **1** Prepare the basic **Cup** shape (page 14).

1

Elephant *continued*

(2) Add hair to the top of the cup, and rub it in to make a larger, higher mound.

(3) Prepare a paper pattern of the ear shape that's about 12 cm (4¾ inches) tall and 8 cm (3⅛ inches) wide. Make two thick sheets of **Gauze** (page 16) that are about 8 mm (¼ inch) thick and cut ears out of them with scissors, using the paper pattern as a guide.

(4) These elephant ears are big and pretty fragile, so reinforce the edges to prevent fraying (see 'Reinforcing Edges', page 19).

(5) For the trunk, make a thick cat-hair **String** (page 18) that is 14 cm (5½ inches) long and 4 cm (1½ inches) thick.

(6) Put the cup on a hat stand while deciding where to put the ears and trunk on the cup. Adjust the shape of the trunk by slightly curving it into an S shape.

(7) Sew the ears and trunk to the cup (see 'Attaching Parts', page 20). Using a longer needle, like a darning needle, will make it easier to attach thick parts like the trunk. While sewing, it's easy to apply too much pressure with the hand holding the cup and crush the hat, so make sure to hold it lightly in your hand.

(8) Roughly rub some cat-hair string together to form two tusks, each 7 cm (2¾ inches) long and 1.5 cm (½ inch) thick. Sharpen one end of each tusk into a point, and cut off the other end with scissors to make it flat.

9 Sew the tusks onto the cup on either side of the base of the trunk, with the pointed ends up and the flat ends flush against the bottom rim of the cup.

10 Make two small balls for the eyes. Crush the two balls flat. For a cute look, you can also simulate sparkle or light reflection in the eye by making two smaller balls out of white or lighter-coloured hair. Position the white balls slightly off-centre on the eye and attach by poking with a felting needle. Then position the eyes on the cup and attach with a felting needle.

11 To make nostrils for the trunk, cut gauze into two oval shapes. Affix them in place with a felting needle.

KOALA

Our cat Nya, who passed away in 2020, looked really good in all of his hats. But the Koala hat, made with his own cat hair, was definitely one of his top three looks!

When I design animal hats, I try to capture the essential characteristics of the animal. Koalas are characterized by their large noses, but their fluffy ears alone are enough to make them recognizable. I think this is a good example of how you can express an animal with small elements without having to incorporate all of the animal's features.

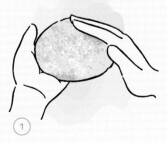

1 Prepare the basic **Cup** shape (page 14).

1

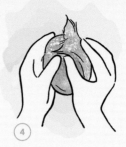

Koala *continued*

(2) To make the ears, place some loose hair between your hands and roll it into a ball that is about 5 cm (2 inches) across. Repeat to form another ball.

(3) Squish the balls between your hands into flat circles. Rubbing the ears between your palms will entangle them and strengthen the shape of the ears.

(4) If the outer edges of the ears are too delicate and fluffy, wrap them with **Gauze** (page 16). If the ears look too small, layer some extra pieces of gauze onto the ears to make them bigger.

(5) To make the ears bushy, create about twenty thin cat-hair **Strings** (page 18) of about 3 cm (1¼ inches) in length. Place one end of each string onto the outer lower edge of the ear and poke the string's end with a felting needle to embed it in the ear.

(6) Rub and press the inner side of each ear to form a dent that will fit the curvature of the cup. If the ear is too stiff to form a dent, use scissors to cut a curved piece out of the ear. You are aiming for an ear shape that is about halfway between a full circle and a semi-circle.

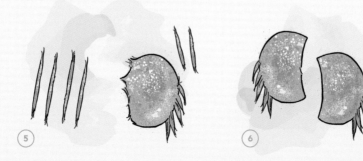

(7) Attach the ears to the cup (see 'Attaching Parts', page 20).

(8) Conceal the joints of the ears (see 'Hiding Seams & Joints', page 22).

(9) Add gauze of different-coloured cat hair on the inner part of the ears for a more realistic, three-dimensional look.

LION

A hat like the Halloween Witch hat (page 73) looks good from any angle but note that most of the time, hats are photographed from the front, so it's okay if the back doesn't look as good. We once made a hat with a bunch of grapes on the front, but the back had no grapes on it. So we just shot the front. The Lion hat is another one that looks better when photographed head on.

(1) Make fluffy cat-hair **Strings** (page 18) that are about 10 cm (4 inches) in length. You'll need enough of these to cover the entire circumference of your cat's face; about forty-five should suffice.

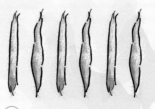

(1)

Lion *continued*

2. Cut a piece of thin rope or yarn to about 50 cm (19½ inches).

3. Wrap one end of a cat-hair string around the rope and then sew it on using a needle and thread.

4. Repeat with the remaining strings.

5. Place the hat around your cat's face and tie the rope in a bow under your cat's chin.

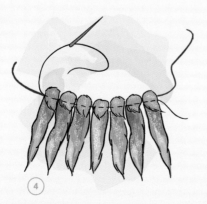

Variation

If you would like your cat to resemble a lion even more, prepare the basic **Cup** shape (page 14). Then use a felting needle to implant a bunch of fluffy cat hair strings all over the cup to cover it like a mane. This version of the hat will definitely look great from a side angle.

SHEEP

Our cat Maru has a very fuzzy body, so when he sits with this hat on, he really looks like an actual sheep. Once you make this hat for your cat, you might start counting cats instead of sheep on sleepless nights!

For hats with parts that extend below the cup, like this one, it is helpful to use a homemade hat stand when assembling the hat (see 'Recommended Tools', page 8).

1 Prepare the basic **Cup** shape (page 14).

1

(2)

(3)

Sheep *continued*

(2) To create the horns, make two thick cat-hair **Strings** (page 18). Keep the root portion thick, and make the tip thin. Curve the horns into a crescent shape. If the horns wrinkle when you curve them, place some **Gauze** (page 16) over the wrinkles and rub it in to hide them.

(3) Sew the horns to the left and right side of the cup (see 'Attaching Parts', page 20). We recommend pulling the thread tightly while sewing so that the horns don't fall off. (Sometimes, when you pull the thread through firmly, dents may appear in the cup. Don't worry too much about this, as you will be adding fluffy balls of hair to the cup, which will hide the dents.)

(4) Make about thirty very fluffy balls of cat hair, handling them lightly so they look like little pieces of candyfloss. Be careful not to make them hard or firm.

(5) Place a ball on the cup and poke the base of the ball a few times with a felting needle to attach it to the cup. Repeat with the remaining balls until the surface of the cup is covered.

(4)   (5)

SNAIL

It might be hard to imagine a cat imitating a snail. But, actually, when cats curl up in a ball and bask in the sun, they do kind of look a bit like snails. This hat was inspired by all those interesting poses cats do from time to time.

When taking photos of this hat on your cat, we recommend placing light blue or green objects around your pet. This can add a rainy-day tone to the photos. Simply by putting a little piece of cloth on a chair nearby, the mood of the photos can change quite dramatically.

① Make the basic **Cup** shape (page 14).

①

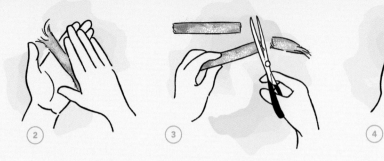

Snail *continued*

(2) For the tentacles (eye stalks), make two stiff pieces of cat-hair **String** (page 18). (A firm string will be more stable when attached to the cup.)

(3) Cut off both fluffy ends of each string so that you're left with the firm centre pieces, each about 8 cm (3⅛ inches) in length.

(4) Rub one end of each string to taper into the shape of a baby corn.

(5) Make two small balls that are about 2 cm (¾ inch) across. Make a small hole in each ball with a sewing needle or scissor tips so that they will fit nicely onto the ends of the tentacles.

(6) Attach the balls to the tips of the tentacles with a felting needle.

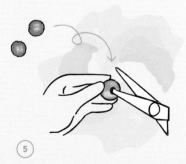

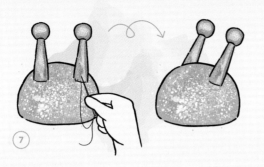
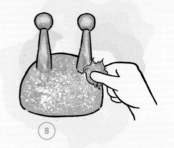

(7)

(8)

(7) Sew the tentacles onto the top of the cup (see 'Attaching Parts', page 20). If you attach the tentacles so that they are tilting forwards a bit, it will really look like a snail.

(8) Conceal the seams and joints of all the attached parts (see 'Hiding Seams & Joints', page 22).

UNICORN

The great thing about cat-hair hats is that they let you transform your cat into legendary creatures quite easily. With this hat, your cat will morph into a mythical unicorn. The primary feature of a unicorn is the long horn growing out of its forehead. Be careful, though – if the horn is made too long, it will be hard to balance the hat on your cat's head. Creating a mane with little curls is the finishing touch for a very cute Unicorn hat.

1 Prepare the basic **Cup** shape (page 14).

1

② ③ ④

Unicorn *continued*

② To make the ears, hold some hair between both hands and roll it into a ball that is about 4 cm (1½ inches) across. Repeat to make a second ball.

③ Hold each ball between your hands and squish it flat. Rub it with your hands while pinching and entwining the hairs together to increase the ear's sturdiness. Pinch one end a bit to make it into a teardrop shape. (The pointy end will be the top of the ear.)

④ Fold each ear in half vertically (lengthways) and rub or push the base of the ear (the rounded end) to dent it a little bit so that the ear fits snugly against the curvature of the cup. If the ear is too firm to make a dent, use scissors to cut it.

⑤ For the horn, make a thick cat-hair **String** (page 18) that is about 14 cm (5½ inches) long and tapers at one end, like a baby corn.

⑥ To make a spiralling groove in the horn, poke it with a felting needle in a line while rotating the horn, so that it looks like a long snail's shell.

⑦ Cut the bottom of the horn with scissors to form a flat surface.

⑤ ⑥ ⑦

(8)

(9)

(8) Decide where to attach the horn and ears on the cup. (If you position the ears facing forwards, the hat will look more like a horse.) Sew the ears and horn to the cup (see 'Attaching Parts', page 20).

(9) For the mane, make about thirty fluffy cat-hair strings of slightly different thicknesses and lengths. (Using strings of various sizes will give the mane better texture and look more realistic.) Apply the base of each string to the cup and pierce it with a felting needle three to five times to embed it in the cup.

(10) Apply different-coloured **Gauze** (page 16) to the inner part of the ears to give them a more realistic, three-dimensional look.

(10)

HATS FOR
HOLIDAYS &
CELEBRATIONS

There are so many holidays and celebrations throughout the year, and the hats in this chapter will help your cat take part in the festivities. Spending quality time with your cat wearing your handmade hat will make for a very special holiday memory.

BIRTHDAY CAKE

Aside from your cat's birthday, the day that you welcomed your cat into your home is also an important day to celebrate. Cakes are a must-have for family birthdays and anniversaries, and you can celebrate your cat with a Birthday Cake hat. You can customize the decorations on this hat to make cakes for different occasions. And, of course, don't forget to give cats their favourite snacks on their special day!

1. To make the moulds needed for this hat, cut two pieces of thick paper: one that is 6 cm (2½ inches) wide and about 38 cm (15 inches) long and another that is 5 cm (2 inches) wide and about 20 cm (8 inches) long.

1

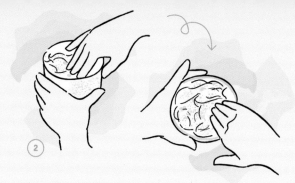

Birthday Cake *continued*

Take the longer piece of paper and tape the ends together to form a ring that is about 12 cm (4¾ inches) across. Use the other to form a second ring that is about 6.5 cm (2⅝ inches) across. (Note that the large ring is the same size mould as used in the Coonskin Cap on page 95, so you can use the same mould for both hats.)

(2) Put the moulds on a flat surface. Fill the larger one to the top with cat hair, pushing down and rubbing as you fill so that the cylinder of hair is firm enough to hold its shape when the mould is removed but not so firm that it's too heavy for your cat. Press the centre in with your fingers or a foam half-sphere to make a dent so your cat's head can fit in it. Fill the smaller mould with cat hair, pushing down to make it firm (you do not need to make a dent in this piece).

(3) Remove the hair from the moulds and stack the smaller layer on top of the larger one. Check the overall balance of the cake. If it looks too tall, cut the lower part of the layers with scissors.

(4) To make decorations for the side of the cake, cut a strip of **Gauze** (page 16) into a pattern of your liking with scissors. For example, we made a strip of gauze with a scalloped pattern on one edge using a paper circle as a guide. You can also make some ribbon from cat-hair **String** (page 18) and use it to make zigzag patterns and/or simple lines.

(5)

(6)

(7)

(5) Attach the decorations to the bottom edge of the lower cake layer by poking them with a felting needle to affix in place.

(6) Sew the upper and lower portions of the cake together with a needle and thread (see 'Attaching Parts', page 20). When sewing thick objects together, it's easiest to use a long darning needle.

(7) Using the same method as described in steps 4 and 5, make and attach the decorations that will go on the upper portion of the cake. Make these decorations a bit smaller to match the size of this layer.

(8) To decorate the top surfaces of the cake, make seven large balls and five small ones by rolling cat hair between your palms. Sew the large balls around the top of the lower cake layer. Sew the small balls around the top of the upper cake layer.

(9) To make a candle, create a thick, solid cat-hair string. Cut both ends flat and make a hole in one end for the flame part.

(10) Stick a small cat-hair string, fashioned into the shape of a flame, into the hole of the candle. Secure it with a felting needle.

(11) Make a hole on the top of the cake with the tip of some scissors and insert the candle to complete the hat.

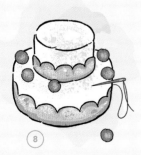

(8)

(9)

(10)

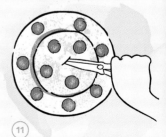

(11)

EASTER BUNNY

This is the first animal hat that umatan ever made for our cats. When she saw our little one with this bunny hat on, she literally screamed because of how cute it was.

You can change the look of the hat by altering the bunny ears. They can be positioned straight up, angled forwards or outwards, flopped down on one or both sides, and more. Try out various positions to see what looks best on your cat.

1 Prepare the basic **Cup** shape (page 14).

1

Easter Bunny *continued*

(2) For the ears, make two thick cat-hair **Strings** (page 18). The length of the ear should be about the same as the diameter of the cup. Round out the side that will become the tip of the ear. Repeat to make the second ear.

(3) Flatten each ear by using both hands. Rub your hands a bit while the ear is sandwiched between them to entangle the hair.

(4) On each ear, push in the base of the ear so that it fits the curve of the cup.

(5) After deciding where the ears will go on the cup, sew the ears to the cup (see 'Attaching Parts', page 20).

(6) Conceal the joints of the ears (see 'Hiding Seams & Joints', page 22).

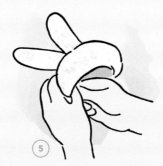

7 To achieve a three-dimensional effect, apply **Gauze** (page 16) made from different-coloured hair on the inside of the ears.

8 Bend the ears to the angle of your choice. You can fold them quite firmly if you poke the inner crease with a felting needle.

GRADUATION CAP

There are only a few universities in Japan that use graduation caps during their ceremonies, but we've always admired the scene of throwing the caps in the air that we see in the movies. Our cats look so wise wearing their mortarboards!

Be careful with how long you make the tassel on the mortarboard. If it's too long, your cat might get excited and start playing with it.

1. Prepare the basic **Cup** shape (page 14).

1

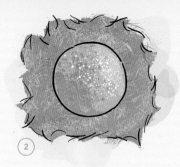

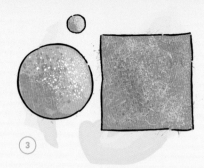

Graduation Cap *continued*

2 For the mortarboard, layer hair onto a piece of **Gauze** (page 16) to make a sheet that is 8 mm (¼ inch) thick. Using scissors, cut the sheet into a square that is the same width and length as the diameter of the cup.

3 Make a small ball and squish it into a disc that is about 3 cm (1¼ inch) across. This will be the button on top of the cap.

4 Make one long cat-hair **String** (page 18), about 20 cm (8 inches) in length, for the tassel. This string can be broken easily, so make it strong and tight.

5 Make five small cat-hair strings, each about 5 cm (2 inches) in length. Tie all five strings to the end of the long string with some thread and a square knot.

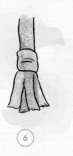

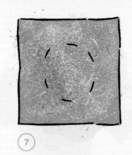

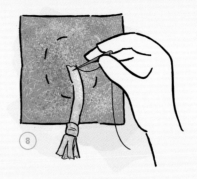

(6) Wrap another short cat-hair string around the join and fasten it closed by poking it with a felting needle.

(7) Sew the mortarboard onto the top of the cup (see 'Attaching Parts', page 20).

(8) Sew the plain end of the tassel string onto the centre of the mortarboard.

(9) Sew the button made in Step 3 in the centre, where the tassel attaches to the mortarboard, which will hide the tassel's seam.

(10) Conceal the seams of thread visible on the top of the mortarboard (see 'Hiding Seams & Joints', page 22).

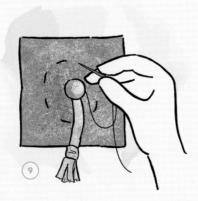

HALLOWEEN WITCH

When Halloween comes around, it's the perfect occasion to enjoy with your cat. Making witch hats for them is a fun activity to celebrate the season. If you make a hat that points straight up, you can transform your cat into a cute and energetic-looking witch. If you bend the hat into a crumpled shape, the cat will look like a wise, accomplished witch. And if you bend the brim so that just one eye peeks out, your cat will look mysterious. Feel free to play around with your creations!

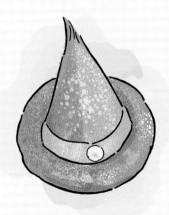

1 Make the basic **Cup** shape (page 14).

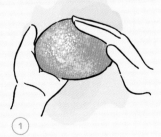

1

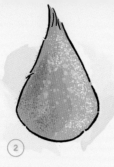
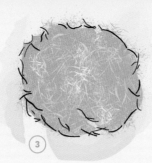
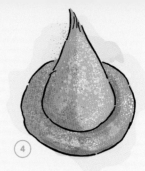

Halloween Witch *continued*

2. Place some extra hair onto the top of the cup and shape it into a cone.

3. To create a brim for the hat, layer some extra hair onto a sheet of **Gauze** (page 16) to make it 8 mm (¼ inch) thick.

4. Place the cone shape on top of the gauze sheet to determine the size of the brim. The brim should extend 5 cm (2 inches) beyond the cone on all sides. Cut the flat sheet into a circle, rub the surface of the brim to smooth it out and reinforce the edges (see 'Reinforcing Edges', page 19).

5. Make a hole in the centre of the brim that is slightly smaller than the base of the cone.

6. Put the cone through the hole, pointy end first, and push the brim down until it is at the base of the cone. The cat hair around the edge of the hole will be pushed up a little around the base of the cone, allowing you to sew the brim onto the cone (see 'Attaching Parts', page 20).

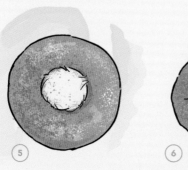

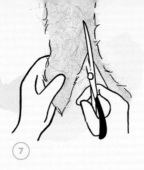

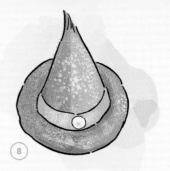

(7) Cut a strip of gauze with scissors to form a hatband that is 2 cm (¾ inch) wide and long enough to encircle the base of the cone. Wrap the band around the base to cover the seams made in Step 6, then rub it a little with your fingertips and poke it here and there with a felting needle to affix.

(8) To create a clasp (optional), make a small ball and squish it down into the shape of a circle or square about the same width as the hatband. Secure it onto the front of the hatband with a felting needle.

SANTA CLAUS

We really like this Santa Claus hat, and umatan has made it at least three times, changing the design a bit each time. Just the sight of Christmas lights on the tree and a fluffy cat with a cute hat on makes us incredibly happy. This hat can be a gift to your cat to thank them for being in your life the entire year. Thanks, little Santa!

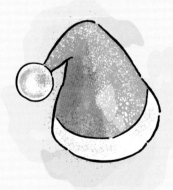

(1) Make the basic **Cup** shape (page 14).

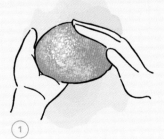

(1)

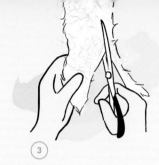

Santa Claus *continued*

(2) Place some hair on top of the cup and rub it into a cone shape.

(3) For the furry base of the hat, use scissors to cut a strip of different-coloured **Gauze** (page 16) that is 4 cm (1½ inches) wide and long enough to encircle the base of the cone. Wrap it around the base like a hatband. Rub the gauze with your fingertips and poke it here and there with a felting needle to affix it in place.

(4) Roll some hair into a ball that is 3 cm (1¼ inches) across and make a hole in the ball using a sewing needle or scissor tips.

(5) Stuff the tip of the cone into the hole of the ball and fasten the ball on with a felting needle.

(6) Gently bend the cone to complete the look.

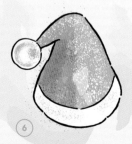

Variation

The Santa Claus hat can be finished as is, but we like to add a few extra Christmas decorations to the mix. Two additional balls can be made to look like berries or baubles, and holly leaves can be made by cutting some gauze with scissors and affixing them to the band with a felting needle. Use your imagination and make as many of your favourite decorations as you'd like!

REINDEER

If you own several cats, it's definitely
more fun to have Santa and a reindeer
or two to liven up your Christmas party!

Mugi the reindeer doesn't deliver
gifts, and he sleeps in cardboard
boxes all the time. But the best gift
for us is his sleeping face!

(1) Make the basic **Cup** shape (page 14).

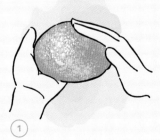

(1)

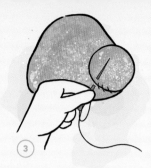

Reindeer *continued*

(2) To make the reindeer's head taller so it will rise above the snout, add extra hair to the top of the cup and rub it in to increase the height by about 1 cm (⅜ inch).

(3) For the snout, hold some cat hair in your hands and roll it into a ball that is about 7 cm (2¾ inches) across. Squish the ball a little and sew it onto the front of the cup (see 'Attaching Parts', page 20). Using a longer needle, like a darning needle, makes it easier to attach big parts. Conceal the joint (see 'Hiding Seams & Joints', page 22).

(4) To make the ears, roll two balls that are each about 4 cm (1½ inches) across. Hold each ball and squish it between your hands. Rub your hands together a bit and squeeze the hairs together to entangle the hair and strengthen the shape. Rub the edges of each ear into the shape of a teardrop.

(5) Fold each ear in half vertically (lengthways). Rub or push the rounded base of the ear to dent it a little so that it fits snugly against the curve of the cup. If the hair is too hard to dent, use scissors to cut it.

(6) To make the antlers, create two thick cat-hair **Strings** (page 18), each about 7 cm (2¾ inches) long and 1.5 cm (½ inch) thick. Poke the tip of each one with a felting needle to make it round and bend the string slightly.

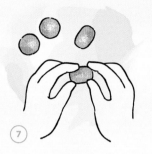

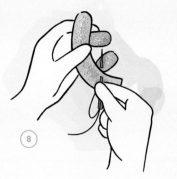

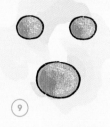

(7) For the branching parts of the antlers, make four small balls that are each 1.5 cm (½ inch) across and squish them into a capsule shape.

(8) Sew two branching parts to the inner curve of each main antler.

(9) Make two balls for the eyes and one for the nose. Flatten them into ovals, about 2 by 1.5 cm (¾ by ½ inch) for the eyes and 4 by 3 cm (1½ by 1¼ inches) for the nose. You can change the reindeer's expression by changing the sizes and positions of the eyes and nose, so try out various options, if you'd like. You can also add a 'sparkle' to the eyes if you wish (see the Elephant hat on page 35, Step 10).

(10) Sew the ears and antlers to the cup and hide the seams and joints.

(11) Fasten the eyes and nose onto the cup with a felting needle.

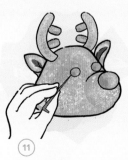

CHARACTERS &

OTHER CURIOUS

HATS

In this chapter, you'll learn to make ambitious hats that transform your cat into characters from history, movies and books, as well as some other amusing hats. With eleven hats to choose from – some adventurous, others elegant or silly – you'll definitely find one that suits your cat's personality. It's your role to play the part of a hat designer, exclusively for cats, and to make your cat a star.

AMELIA EARHART

This hat could be a racing helmet or an old-fashioned flight cap for an aviator like Amelia Earhart. You can finish off the outfit with a jaunty red scarf made from a scrap of fabric. In Japan, the main character in the *Kamen Rider* sci-fi action series for kids always wore a red scarf. So, for us on this side of the world, a red scarf is a sign of a hero's courage in the face of difficulties.

1 Make the basic **Cup** shape (page 14).

1

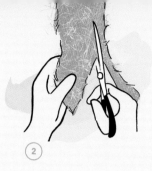

(2)

(3)

(4)

Amelia Earhart *continued*

(2) Make a piece of **Gauze** (page 16) and cut it with scissors to make a ribbon or ribbons of whatever width you like. (We used one large centre stripe flanked by two thinner ones, but you can be creative.) Place the stripes across the top of the cup, running from front to back, and rub them in lightly.

(3) For the decorative trim around the edge, use scissors to cut a strip of gauze that is 2 cm (¾ inch) wide and long enough to wrap around the bottom of the cup. Wrap it around the base of the cup, rub the gauze with your fingertips to attach it, and then poke it with a felting needle to secure it.

(4) To create the goggle lenses, make two balls and squish them into a flat oval shape.

(5) For the frame, make a thin, tight cat-hair **String** (page 18), and place it along the edge of the lenses. Sew the frame onto the edge of the lenses with a needle and thread, and then rub the ends of the thread into the back of the lenses to anchor them.

(6) Sew the goggles onto the front of the cup along the trim (see 'Attaching Parts', page 20), leaving a little space between the two lenses.

(7) Form the nose bridge between the lenses by placing a small piece of cat-hair string between the two lenses. Carefully tuck the ends of the string under the rims of the lenses and affix the string in place by poking it a few times with a felting needle.

(5)

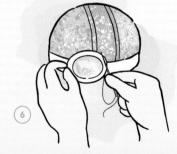

(6)

(7)

Variation

If you attach earmuffs to both sides of this hat, it will look even more like a flight cap. Crush two balls of cat hair into the shape of some earmuffs, and sew them onto the sides of the cup (see 'Attaching Parts', page 20).

CHEESEHEAD

It's difficult to make straight sides with cat hair, so the Cheesehead hat is made by first building a mould out of cardboard and then filling it with hair.

The Cheesehead is also tricky to photograph because the hat tends to look like a flat object in photos. To make it look three-dimensional, adjust the angle of your shot so that there are shadows in the cheese holes.

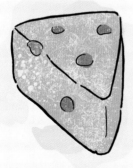

1. To make the mould, cut a strip of cardboard that is about 10 cm (4 inches) wide by 57 cm (22½ inches) long. Fold the length of the cardboard into a triangle with two sides that are each 20 cm (8 inches) and one short side that is about 17 cm (6¾ inches) in length. Tape the ends together. Cat-hair hats will swell up and get bigger as time goes by, so make the mould a little smaller than the exact size hat you want to make.

1

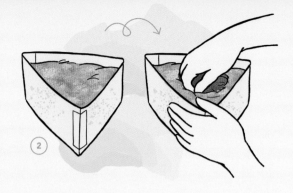

Cheesehead *continued*

2 Set the mould on a flat surface and fill it to the top with cat hair, pushing down and rubbing as you fill so that the hair is firm enough to hold its shape when the mould is removed. Press the centre in with your fingers or a foam half-sphere to make a dent large enough to fit your cat's head.

3 Remove the mould and continue to shape the hat. Add some extra hair or some **Gauze** (page 16) to repair any bumpy parts.

4 To make some holes in the cheese, slowly push the surface in with your finger or a needle to make a dent. If the hair is too dense to make dents, use scissors to cut shallow holes into the hair.

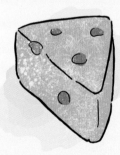

COONSKIN CAP

The trademark of a coonskin cap is a large raccoon tail, and the hat may tilt because of the weight of this part. Make a deeper than usual dent for your cat's head so the hat can be worn a bit lower and it will be more stable. The connection between the hat and tail is fragile, so treat it with care.

When taking photos, don't let the tail fall completely behind your cat's head or it will hit the cat's back and break.

1 To make the mould, cut a piece of thick paper that is 6 cm (2½ inches) wide and about 38 cm (15 inches) long. Tape the two ends together to form a ring that is about 12 cm (4¾ inches) across. (This is the same size as the bottom of the Birthday Cake hat on page 61, so you can use the same mould for both hats.)

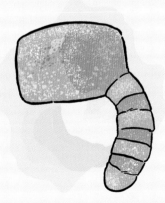

1

Coonskin Cap *continued*

(2) Put the ring on a flat surface and fill the mould to the top with hair, pushing down and rubbing as you fill so that the cylinder of hair is firm enough to hold its shape when the mould is removed. Press the centre in with your fingers or a foam half-sphere, making a dent deep enough to allow the hat to sit low on your cat's head.

(3) Remove the cat hair from the mould. Add hair or use **Gauze** (page 16) to repair any bumpy or misshapen parts.

(4) For the raccoon tail, make a thick cat-hair **String** (page 18) that is about 20 cm (8 inches) long and 5 cm (2 inches) wide. Rub the string hard to make it as firm as possible. Taper and round the bottom end like the tip of a raccoon tail. Be careful that the tail isn't too long – if it is, whenever your cat sits, the tail will hit the floor. (Note that the top 5 cm [2 inches] of the tail will be sewn into the hat.)

(5) For the tail stripes, cut some different-coloured gauze into ribbons. Leaving the top 5 cm (2 inches) of the tail blank, wrap the ribbons around the remaining length of the tail at intervals. Attach them by poking with a felting needle.

(6) Sew the top 5 cm (2 inches) of the tail to the outside of the hat with a needle and thread (see 'Attaching Parts', page 20). The tail can become detached quite easily, so make sure it's firmly affixed.

(7) Cover any seams (see 'Hiding Seams & Joints', page 22) and irregularities with more cat hair and blend it in.

FLOWER WREATH

Our cats look incredibly cute when wearing the Flower Wreath. The flowers on this wreath are made using a crepe silk handicraft technique that's traditionally done with Japanese cloth. They are designed to look like the blossoms of an ume, a Japanese fruit tree that is similar to a plum or apricot. You can use this flower not only for the wreath but to decorate other hats as well.

① To figure out the length of cat-hair string needed for the wreath, wrap a cord or ribbon around your cat's head like a headband and mark the spot where the cord meets the end. Measure that length.

①

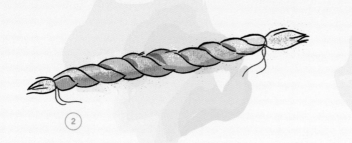

Flower Wreath *continued*

(2) For the wreath base, make two firm cat-hair **Strings** (page 18) that are each the length you measured in Step 1 plus an extra 5 cm (2 inches). Twist the strings together into a rope while being careful not to tear them. Tie both ends with some thread to secure the twist. You could also use a strip of lace ribbon for your wreath base instead of cat-hair strings for a cute look.

(3) Make a firm ball by rolling cat hair between your palms. Crush the ball into a little disc with a diameter of 2.5 to 4 cm (1 to 1½ inches). Make another pea-sized ball to be used as the centre of the flower.

(4) To turn the disc into a flower, start by threading a needle with some thread that's a bright, contrasting colour to the cat hair. Don't tie a knot at the end of the thread; just pierce the centre of the disc from the back and pull the thread almost all the way through, leaving 5 to 7.5 cm (2 or 3 inches) hanging like a little tail. As you continue sewing, hold onto this tail firmly so that it doesn't pull through.

(5) Draw the thread over and around the edge of the disc, and then poke the needle through the centre of the back to the front once again. Pull the thread tight so that it forms an indent in the edge of the disc. Repeat this process five times, moving around the edge of the disc to make five petals.

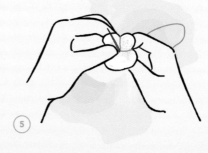

(6)   When you complete the final petal threading, pierce the pea-sized ball with the needle and sew back down through the centre of the flower to attach it.

(7)   Tie the two ends of the thread into a square knot that is flush against the back of the flower.

(8)   Measure the flower, and then calculate how many more flowers you need to fill your wreath. You'll want to sandwich the flowers pretty closely together to make this design. (An easier option, if you don't want to make so many flowers, is to alternate flowers with little balls of hair.)

(9)   Sew the flowers onto the wreath base, leaving 2.5 cm (1 inch) empty at each end of the base.

(10) Overlap the two ends of the base and sew them together securely to make a nice ring. Add a final flower onto the empty spot.

(11) To decorate the wreath with leaves, crush a few 3-cm (1¼-inch) pieces of string into leaf shapes. Tuck the base of each leaf behind a flower and poke with a felting needle to attach to the back of the flowers.

JESTER

We originally made this cap to represent the joker when our cats and their hats were featured on a set of playing cards! A jester would normally wear a quirky outfit to go with the hat, but our cats are not too good with wearing clothes. However, our cats can wear collars, so I hand-made an amusing collar fit for a joker.

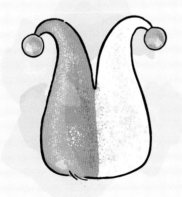

1. Make the basic **Cup** shape (page 14) with one colour of cat hair.

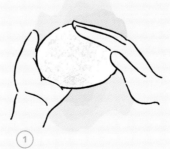

1

Jester *continued*

(2) To create each prong of the hat, make two very thick cat-hair **Strings** (page 18) that are about 4 cm (1½ inches) thick and 20 cm (8 inches) long. Rub them firmly. Sharpen one end of each into a tip, and cut the other end with scissors to fit against the curve of the cup. If you want a two-toned hat, make each cone a different colour.

(3) Sew the cones onto the cup (see 'Attaching Parts', page 20).

(4) Bend the tip of each cone slightly out and away from the front of the hat.

(5) If one of your cones is a different colour from the cup, cover half the cup with some **Gauze** (page 16) to match the colour of the cone.

(6) Conceal the seams and joints (see 'Hiding Seams & Joints', page 22).

(7) Make two balls that are each 3 cm (1¼ inches) across. Poke a hole in each ball with the tip of a dressmaking pin or scissors. Place the tip of each cone in the hole of the ball and affix it with a felting needle.

Variation

We've made a two-pronged jester hat. If you want to make a three-
or four-pronged hat (see the photo above), just make extra cones
and add them to the cup. It may look even wackier on your cat!

PRINCESS LEIA

Transforming your cat into a character from a movie is always fun! How about enjoying Star Wars Day (May the fourth) while your cat plays a starring role as Princess Leia? There are many hairstyles in the *Star Wars* universe, so the next time you watch a *Star Wars* film or show, make sure to keep an eye out for other good ideas and 'May the fur be with you!'

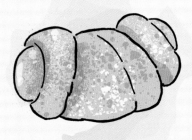

(1) Prepare the basic **Cup** shape (page 14).

(1)

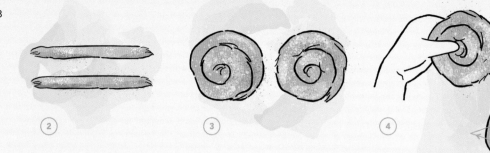

Princess Leia *continued*

(2) Make two thick cat-hair **Strings** (page 18) of about 30 cm (12 inches) in length.

(3) Twist the cat-hair strings and roll them into spirals like two cinnamon buns.

(4) Stitch the underside of the spiral shapes so that they don't unravel. If you skewer the spirals with needle and thread, going through the spirals from the sides in the pattern of a five-pointed star, they will hold their form. As you start to sew, leave a 10-cm (4-inch) tail of thread hanging loose, and then finish sewing near your starting point, leaving another 10-cm (4-inch) tail of thread. Tie the two ends of thread together in a square knot.

(5) Sew the two spiral shapes onto the sides of the cup (see 'Attaching Parts', page 20).

(6) To create a centre parting in the hairstyle, take a felting needle and poke repeatedly in a line down the middle of the cup.

PROPELLER BEANIE

In Japan, there is a flying gadget called a Hopter that is similar to a beanie hat that appears in the very famous anime *Doraemon*. When umatan was little, she used to dream that she could use a Hopter to get to school. Now she finally has a hat with a propeller, but this cat-hair hat is too light and she feels like it will blow away at any moment!

Maybe when your cats wear the Propeller Beanie, they will dream of flying too.

1   Make the basic **Cup** shape (page 14).

1

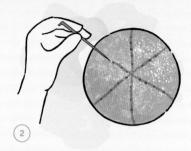

Propeller Beanie *continued*

(2) If you want separate colours (optional) on the surface of the cup, use a felting needle to poke lines or borders in the cup, dividing it into six triangular sections.

(3) Make six thin cat-hair **Strings** (page 18). Place them along the borders of the areas that will be coloured in and fasten them lightly by poking with a felting needle. Use scissors to cut any excess hanging over the edge.

(4) Take small pieces of different-coloured **Gauze** (page 16) and rub the gauze into the triangular areas that lie between the borders to make it stick. In the Propeller Beanie shown here, three colours are alternated to make six distinct panels. Four of the panels (two colours) are made of rubbed-on gauze, while the remaining two panels are simply the base colour of the cup.

(5) To create a brim for the hat, make a thick piece of gauze that is about 8 mm (¼ inch) thick.

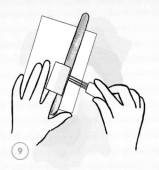

⑦   ⑧   ⑨

6 With scissors, cut out the shape of a curved brim that is about 14 cm (5½ inches) long by 6 cm (2½ inches) wide at the widest part of the curve. Reinforce the edge of the curved brim (see 'Reinforcing Edges', page 19).

7 For the shaft that connects the cup and propeller, make a firm cat-hair string that is about 12 cm (4¾ inches) long.

8 For the propeller, prepare a firm cat-hair string that is about the same length as the diameter of the cup, about 10 cm (4 inches). Squish it flat and then round off the ends.

9 Reinforce the edges of the propeller (page 19).

10 Wrap 5 cm (2 inches) of the shaft around the centre of the propeller, and sew the end of the shaft down to secure the propeller in place.

11 Sew the brim onto the front of the cup (see 'Attaching Parts', page 20).

12 Make a hole in the top of the cup with the tip of your scissors, insert about 2 cm (¾ inch) of the propeller into the cup, and affix it in place with a felting needle.

⑩   ⑪   ⑫

QUEEN

Being able to make a wig out of your own hair is quite a strange idea, but maybe humans will covet this wig-making technique for themselves when they see the elegant Queen hat. You can add a lace collar to your cat for a regal finishing touch.

For hats with parts that extend below the cup, like this one, it's helpful to use a homemade hat stand when assembling the hat (see 'Recommended Tools', page 8).

(1) Prepare the basic **Cup** shape (page 14).

(1)

2

3

4

Queen *continued*

2   For the wig, make about forty fluffy
cat-hair **Strings** (page 18) of varying
thicknesses. Since one end of each string
will be the tip of the hair, make sure to
twist and thin out those ends.

3   Apply the root of each string to the cup,
and pierce the root with a felting needle
three to five times to embed it in the cup.
Repeat until the cup's surface is covered
with strings.

4   To create the plait, make three thick
cat-hair strings that are each about
15 cm (6 inches) long. Plait the three
strings together. Tie the two ends of the
plait with thread to secure them.

5   To make a bow for the end of the plait,
form a ball about the size of a ping-
pong ball. Squeeze the ball between
your palms to flatten it. Pinch the centre,
wrap a long thread around the centre,
and tie it. Rub it with your finger to set
the shape of the bow. Tie the bow to
the plait with thread.

6   To make the crown, prepare a ball that
is about 6 cm (2½ inches) across. Place it
on a flat surface and squish it a bit so it's
the shape of a steamed pork bun.

7   Make six equidistant grooves on the
surface of the crown, running from
the base to a central point on top,
by poking repeatedly in a line with
a felting needle.

5

6

7

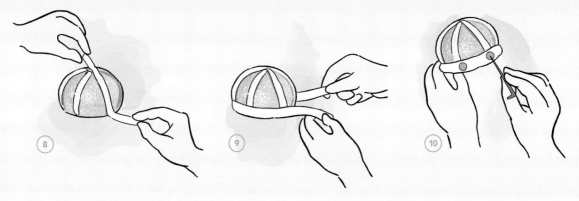

8. Make three small strings using cat hair of a different colour. Place the strings along the grooves and fasten each one lightly by poking with a felting needle. Cut off any extra string with scissors.

9. To make a band for the edge of the crown, prepare a cat-hair string that is long enough to wrap around the base of the crown. Flatten the string so it is about 1.5 cm (½ inch) thick. Wrap the band around the crown and fasten it in place by sewing in a zigzag pattern.

10. To decorate the crown band, create six small balls that are each about 1 cm (⅜ inch) across. Squish to flatten just a bit. (They are cuter when they are left a little plump.) Using a felting needle, fasten the decorations onto the crown band at the base of each cat-hair string.

11. For the cone-shaped adornment at the top of the crown, make a ball that is about 2 cm (¾ inch) across and knead it into a cone shape. Place it on top of the crown, and secure it with a felting needle.

12. Before finishing the hat, try the wig on your cat to position the fringe, plait and crown properly. Be careful not to block your cat's field of vision with the plait. Place the wig on the hat stand and sew the plait onto the inside of the cup with a needle and thread. Sew the crown onto the wig in the same way.

SHERLOCK HOLMES

This Sherlock Holmes hat is perfect for detectives. Your first job as an assistant detective is to make the hat. Afterwards, you and your cat can start investigating mysteries around the house.

A traditional deerstalker hat has a brim on the back as well, but we won't make it for this hat, as it would touch your cat's back and break because it's fragile.

1 Make the basic **Cup** shape (page 14).

1

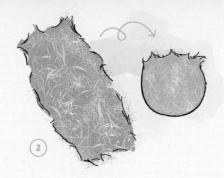

(2)   (3)   (4)

Sherlock Holmes *continued*

(2) To create a brim for the hat, make some **Gauze** (page 16) into a thick sheet that is about 8 mm (¼ inch) thick. Using scissors, cut it into the shape of a curved brim about 14 cm (5½ inches) long by 6 cm (2½ inches) wide at the widest part of the curve.

(3) Make another sheet of thick gauze for the two ear flaps, which will be in the shape of tombstones. The flat bottom edge of each ear flap will be folded under the rim of the cup, while the top rounded edges of the flaps will nearly touch on top of the cup. Measure the ear flaps accordingly (you may want to make a paper pattern to ensure you have the correct size), and then cut the flaps from the sheet of gauze.

(4) Cover the fluffy portions of the brim and ear flaps with some extra gauze and, if necessary, reinforce the edges (see 'Reinforcing Edges', page 19) to strengthen these parts.

(5) Sew the brim onto the cup (see 'Attaching Parts', page 20).

(6) Sew the bottom of the ear flaps to the inside of the cup, and then sew the tips of the ear flaps near the top of the cup.

(7) For the ribbon, make one cat-hair **String** (page 18) that is about 20 cm (8 inches) long and two shorter strings that are about 8 cm (3⅛ inches).

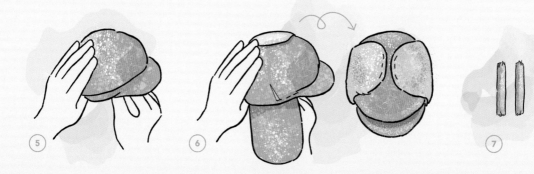

(5)   (6)   (7)

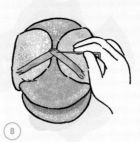

8. Place the two small strings onto the top of the cup and affix them in place by poking the ends into the cup with a felting needle.

9. Make a ring with the long string and pinch the centre to form a figure-eight shape for the bow. Sew the centre of this shape so that it doesn't come loose.

10. Sew the bow shape to the top of the hat.

11. To make the seams of the hat, create a groove down the front of the cap by poking the surface with a felting needle.

TOP HAT

The Top Hat always made our beloved Nya look dandy! He was so dignified and charming in it that the hat became synonymous with Nya in our minds. Just as specific clothes or colours suit certain humans, some unique hats will definitely suit particular cats. What kind of hat looks great on your cat? It's always fun trying to find out.

1   For the mould, cut a thick piece of paper that is 9 cm (3½ inches) wide and about 32 cm (12½ inches) long. Form a ring with the paper that is about 10 cm (4 inches) across, and tape it together.

1

Top Hat *continued*

(2) Put the mould on a flat surface and fill it to the top with cat hair, pushing down and rubbing as you fill so that the cylinder of hair is firm enough to hold its shape when the mould is removed. Press the centre in with your fingers or a foam half-sphere to make a dent large enough to fit your cat's head.

(3) Remove the cat hair from the mould, and shape it into a cylinder. If it is bumpy and misshapen, add some additional hair or **Gauze** (page 16) and rub it in to make it smooth.

(4) To make the brim, layer some extra hair onto a sheet of gauze until it is 8 mm (¼ inch) thick.

(5) Place the cylinder on top of this thick gauze sheet to determine the size of the brim; it should extend 4 cm (1½ inches) from the cylinder on all sides. Use scissors to cut the circular brim from the gauze. To prevent fluffing, rub or reinforce the cut edges (see 'Reinforcing Edges', page 19).

(6) In the centre of the circular brim, make a hole that is slightly smaller than the base of your cylinder.

(7) Slide the brim down onto the cylinder from the top of the hat until it's in its final position. The cat hair around the edge of the hole will be pushed up a little around the base of the cylinder, allowing you to sew the brim onto the cylinder with a needle and thread (see 'Attaching Parts', page 20).

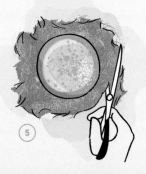

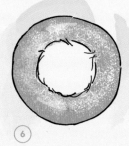

8 For the hatband, make gauze and cut it with scissors into a strip that is 2 cm (¾ inch) wide and long enough to wrap around the cylinder. Wrap the band around the base of the cylinder and prick it with a felting needle to secure it.

9 You can leave the brim straight or curve up the edges as much as you like. The brim bends with just a light push of your finger, so you can try out various styles while taking photos with your cat to see what looks best.

VIKING HELMET

This is definitely the coolest and most powerful-looking hat in this book! It's fun to make the horns as big as possible and to add some plaits, too. This hat will last longer and be more stable if you stuff the hair tightly into the cup and make the roots of the horns thick.

① Make the basic **Cup** shape (see page 14). Because this hat has a lot of parts and large pieces, which can damage the cup, it's important to make the cup really strong.

①

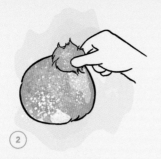

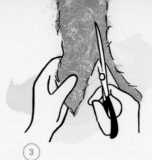

Viking Helmet *continued*

(2) Add extra hair to the top of the cup to strengthen it and make a larger, higher mound.

(3) To make some helmet ornamentation, prepare a thick strip of **Gauze** (page 16). Cut it to make two long ribbons that are each 2 cm (¾ inch) wide and long enough to wrap around the cup.

(4) Centre the first ribbon over the top of the cup, poke it lightly with a felting needle to secure it, and trim off any excess with scissors. Wrap the second ribbon around the edge of the cup and poke it lightly with a felting needle to secure.

(5) For the spike at the top of the helmet, make a firm cat-hair **String** (page 18) by rubbing the string hard. Sharpen one end into a point and use scissors to cut the other end flat. The height of the spike should be about 3.5 cm (1⅜ inches).

(6) For the horns, make two very thick cat-hair strings that are about 4 cm (1½ inches) thick and 20 cm (8 inches) long. Rub them firmly.

(7) Sharpen one end of each horn into a tip and bend the horns a little for a better shape. Cut the other end of the horns diagonally so that they fit against the sides of the cup. Sew them onto the sides of the cup (see 'Attaching Parts', page 20).

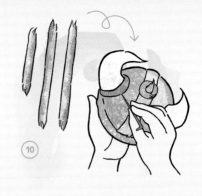

(8) Make four pea-sized balls and crush them into buttons. Affix them onto the centre ribbon by poking them with a felting needle, with two buttons on the front and two on the back of the helmet.

(9) Make a hole in the top of the helmet with the tip of your scissors. Insert the spike and affix it in place with a felting needle.

(10) Prepare three cat-hair strings, one short and two long. Wrap the short one around the base of the spike and wrap the two long ones around the bases of the horns. Affix all three with a felting needle.

(11) If you want to add plaits (optional), make six cat-hair strings that are each about 23 cm (9 inches) long. Divide the strings into two sets of three and weave into two plaits. To keep the plaits from unravelling, tie each end with a thread. Sew the plaits onto the inside of the cup, on the left and right sides.

(12) Cover the seams and any bumps with gauze to smooth the surface (see 'Hiding Seams & Joints', page 22).

ABOUT THE CATS

Nya

Type Male Scottish Fold

Birthday b. 14/02/2007, d. 09/04/2020

Fur colour Blue-grey tabby

Eye colour Green

Favourite thing Licking water droplets on a glass

Thing he hated Cat litter

We welcomed Nya into our home the year we got married. He had a friendly personality that you could feel as he passed by your feet or sat next to you. Nya had clear eyes and a cute nose, so hats looked very cool on him. He was our eldest son and could always be relied on for good photos whenever his younger brothers were being fussy with the hats. Nya had a very fluffy coat that actually did not shed much, even during seasonal moulting periods. His hair was so beautiful with its grey gradient.

Maru

Type Male Scottish Fold

Birthday 27/03/2009

Fur colour White

Eye colour Yellow

Favourite thing Catnip toy doll

Thing he hates Guests

Maru is a greedy cat who eats both his and his brother's food – he is our resident dish cleaner. He is incredibly shy, and whenever strangers visit he squeezes into small spaces to hide. Cute hats look good on him, but he messes most hats up due to his big head. Maru's long hair sheds year round, and because of him we can stock up a lot of cat hair.

Mugi

Type Male Scottish Fold

Birthday 21/02/2014

Fur colour Orange tabby

Eye colour Orange

Favourite thing Smelling Maru's rear end

Thing he hates Having his ears cleaned

Our youngest child, Mugi, likes toys shaped like bees and often runs around the room. Since his head is round like a ball, hats sit well on his head and are quite stable. Mugi is from the same breeder as Maru, so they're related. However, they don't look much alike except for maybe their noses. Mugi has a shiny coat, and the hair he sheds holds some moisture, so his hair is best for the hats. The hats that are made from Mugi's hair last the longest.

Mugi

Maru

Nya

ABOUT THE AUTHORS

rojiman Cat Photographer | @rojiman | The Cat Dad

The resident cat photographer for the family, rojiman is a businessman who usually works from home. He spent his childhood thinking that he loved only dogs, but his entire world flipped upside-down when he met Nya the cat. It was love at first sight. His interest in photography began because he wanted to capture all the wonderful looks cats give us – he is fascinated by the facial expressions of cats and all their sassy gestures. To document his cats' day-to-day moments, rojiman posts daily pics on Instagram.

umatan Cat-Hair Hat Designer | @umatan | The Cat Mum

Whether she's walking around the city or just watching television, umatan finds inspiration for her cat-hair hats everywhere and every day. She started making cat-hair hats in 2016. People often think she's quite skilled with her hands, but in fact she's not very good at sewing. Once when she was a student, she couldn't sew an apron for a home economics class, so she taped the fabric together and handed it in. She works as an editor, and her dream is one day to create a cat magazine.

ACKNOWLEDGEMENTS

The first email we ever received from our editor, Lisa Regul, was in December 2019. She already had a concrete plan for the book in her head and told us the steps we needed to take to make it happen. Immediately after that, however, came the deadly coronavirus. We were worried that we couldn't continue with the project, but she told us, 'We need a book to make people happy,' and her sincere thoughts had a huge impact on us.

Once, at a group cat photo exhibition, we were watching the reaction of the visitors looking at the photos of our cat-hair hats. They seemed to be enjoying themselves, laughing and being surprised at the sight of cats wearing hats. From that experience, we were convinced that what Lisa said about the book was true, and we could make many people happy by making this book.

A number of people made this book a reality. Let us take this opportunity to express our gratitude. Miko Yamanouchi, who followed every step of the contract and encouraged us with some strong words whenever we were worried. Ian Fabian, the translator, who went to great lengths to understand what we wanted. Marisa Kwek drew many illustrations of cat hair and umatan's hands for this book. Her other artwork is colourful and very cheerful, so you should definitely check it out. Generous thanks to Dr Masashi Inoue, a veterinarian and director of Family Animal Hospital in Tokyo, for his professional advice on health and safety when handling cat hair. Christina Spiegel, who first found us and sent our photos to Lisa Regul, is an artist with a very fashionable touch. We are very grateful to have been connected with Lisa through her. And, of course, Lisa. Thank you for finding us among the countless creators scattered across the world. Also, thanks to all the staff members at Ten Speed Press who were involved with this book, including designer Isabelle Gioffredi, art director Kelly Booth and production manager Dan Myers.

Nya

Thank you to everyone who picked this book up. I wholeheartedly hope that you smile with every page you turn.

Finally, we've heard from people who wished they'd heard about cat-hair hats before their pet passed away. We knew that shed hair could always be kept as a memento, but after we lost Nya in April 2020, we realized what that truly meant. Shed cat hair stays warm and soft, just like the cats who shed it. When you make these hats, memories tend to come back while touching the hair, just like when you were petting your cat. Shed hair is a gift from our cats that can connect us with the memories of lost loved ones.

Thank you always to our favourite little ones Nya, Maru and Mugi.

INDEX

HarperCollins*Publishers*
1 London Bridge Street
London SE1 9GF

www.harpercollins.co.uk

HarperCollins*Publishers*
1st Floor, Watermarque Building, Ringsend Road
Dublin 4, Ireland

Published by Pavilion, an imprint of HarperCollins*Publishers* 2022

10 9 8 7 6 5 4 3 2 1

© Hiromi Yamazaki and Ryo Yamazaki 2022
Published by arrangement with Ten Speed Press, an imprint of Random
House, a division of Penguin Random House LLC.
Photographs copyright © 2022 by Hiromi Yamazaki and Ryo Yamazaki
Illustrations except as noted below copyright © 2022 by Marisa Kwek

English translation by Ian Fabian
Illustrations on page 133 by esk

Hiromi Yamazaki and Ryo Yamazaki assert the moral right to be identified as
the authors of this work

A catalogue record of this book is available from the British Library

ISBN 978-0-00-858680-5

Printed and bound in Latvia

All rights reserved. No part of this publication may be reproduced, stored in
a retrieval system, or transmitted, in any form or by any means, electronic,
mechanical, photocopying, recording or otherwise, without the prior written
permission of the publishers.

This book is produced from independently certified FSC™ paper to ensure
responsible forest management.
For more information visit: www.harpercollins.co.uk/green